D1275457

LIVING WITH
RELIGION AND FAITH

Other Books in the LIVING PROUD! Series

LIVING WITH RELIGION AND FAITH

Robert Rodi and Laura Ross

Foreword by Kevin Jennings
Founder, GLSEN (the Gay, Lesbian & Straight
Education Network)

MASON CREST

Mason Crest
450 Parkway Drive, Suite D
Broomall, PA 19008
www.masoncrest.com

Printed in the United States of America

First printing
9 8 7 6 5 4 3 2 1

Series ISBN: 978-1-4222-3501-0
Hardcover ISBN: 978-1-4222-3507-2
ebook ISBN: 978-1-4222-8380-6

Cataloging-in-Publication Data is available on file at the Library of Congress.

Developed and Produced by Print Matters Productions, Inc. (www.printmattersinc.com)
Cover and Interior Design by Kris Tobiassen, Matchbook Digital

Picture credits: 10, Ivan Cholakov/iStock; 22, DNY59/iStock; 26, Lisafx/iStock; 30, lev radin/Shutterstock; 33, Flemming Hansen/iStock; 36, Leskovsek Matej/SIPA/Newscom; 40, Bikeworldtravel/iStock; 44, kaetana_istock/iStock; 48, JulieanneBirch/iStock; 50, mrsixinthemix/iStock; 53, Wikimedia Creative Commons
Front cover: PonyWang/iStock

LIVING WITH
RELIGION AND FAITH

CONTENTS

KEY ICONS TO LOOK FOR

Text-Dependent Questions: These questions send the reader back to the text for more careful attention to the evidence presented there.

Words to Understand: These words with their easy-to-understand definitions will increase the reader's understanding of the text while building vocabulary skills.

Series Glossary of Key Terms: This back-of-the-book glossary contains terminology used throughout this series. Words found here increase the reader's ability to read and comprehend higher-level books and articles in this field.

Research Projects: Readers are pointed toward areas of further inquiry connected to each chapter. Suggestions are provided for projects that encourage deeper research and analysis.

Sidebars: This boxed material within the main text allows readers to build knowledge, gain insights, explore possibilities, and broaden their perspectives by weaving together additional information to provide realistic and holistic perspectives.

FOREWORD

I loved libraries as a kid.

Every Saturday my mom and I would drive from the trailer where we lived on an unpaved road in the unincorporated town of Lewisville, North Carolina, and make the long drive to the "big city" of Winston-Salem to go to the downtown public library, where I would spend joyous hours perusing the books on the shelves. I'd end up lugging home as many books as my arms could carry and generally would devour them over the next seven days, all the while eagerly anticipating next week's trip. The library opened up all kinds of worlds to me—all kinds of worlds, except a gay one.

Oh, I found some "gay" books, even in the dark days of the 1970s. I'm not sure how I did, but I found my way to authors like Tennessee Williams, Yukio Mishima, and Gore Vidal. While these great artists created masterpieces of literature that affirmed that there were indeed other gay people in the universe, their portrayals of often-doomed gay men hardly made me feel hopeful about my future. It was better than nothing, but not much better. I felt so lonely and isolated I attempted to take my own life my junior year of high school.

In the 35 years since I graduated from high school in 1981, much has changed. Gay–straight alliances (an idea my students and I pioneered at Concord Academy in 1988) are now widespread in American schools. Out LGBT (lesbian, gay, bisexual, and transgender) celebrities and programs with LGBT themes are commonplace on the airwaves. Oregon has a proud bisexual governor, multiple members of Congress are out as lesbian, gay, or bisexual, and the White House was bathed in rainbow colors the day marriage equality became the law of the land in 2015. It gets better, indeed.

So why do we need the Living Proud! series?

- Because GLSEN (the Gay, Lesbian & Straight Education Network) reports that over two-thirds of LGBT students routinely hear anti-LGBT language at school.

- Because GLSEN reports that over 60% of LGBT students do not feel safe at school.
- Because the CDC (the Centers for Disease Control and Prevention, a U.S. government agency) reports that lesbian and gay students are four times more likely to attempt suicide than heterosexual students

In my current role as the executive director of the Arcus Foundation (the world's largest financial supporter of LGBT rights), I work in dozens of countries and see how far there still is to go. In over 70 countries same-sex relations are crimes under existing laws: in 8, they are a crime punishable by the death penalty. It's better, but it's not all better—especially in our libraries, where there remains a need for books that address LGBT issues that are appropriate for young people, books that will erase both the sense of isolation so many young LGBT people still feel as well as the ignorance so many non-LGBT young people have, ignorance that leads to the hate and violence that still plagues our community, both at home and abroad.

The Living Proud! series will change that and will save lives. By providing accurate, age-appropriate information to young people of all sexual orientations and gender identities, the Living Proud! series will help young people understand the complexities of the LGBT experience. Young LGBT people will see themselves in its pages, and that reflection will help them see a future full of hope and promise. I wish Living Proud! had been on the shelves of the Winston-Salem/Forsyth County Public Library back in the seventies. It would have changed my life. I'm confident that it will have as big an impact on its readers today as it would have had on me back then. And I commend it to readers of any age.

Kevin Jennings
Founder, GLSEN (the Gay, Lesbian & Straight Education Network)
Executive Director, Arcus Foundation

GLSEN®

GLSEN is the leading national education organization focused on ensuring safe and affirming schools for all students. GLSEN seeks to develop school climates where difference is valued for the positive contribution it makes to creating a more vibrant and diverse community. www.glsen.org

More and more religious institutions are welcoming LGBT worshippers.

ALL ARE WELCOME

1

SEXUAL ORIENTATION AND RELIGION

 WORDS TO UNDERSTAND

Rabbi: A Jewish religious leader.
Mosque: A Muslim place of worship.
Liberal: Open to change and new ideas.
Reincarnation: The belief that souls are reborn in new bodies again and again until they reach enlightenment.
Karma: The force, recognized by both Hindus and Buddhists, that emanates from one's actions in this life; the concept that the good and bad things one does determine where he or she will end up in the next life.

Lauren has always loved church. She appreciates singing the songs, praying, and reading the Bible. Growing up, she loved the feeling she always had at church of connecting to God with a group of other people who worshipped Him in the same way.

But Lauren isn't sure how she feels anymore. As a teenager, she's realized she is a lesbian—and her church has no place in its pews for homosexuals. She can either deny the reality of her sexual orientation or she can leave her church, condemned as a sinner living outside Christ's salvation.

Lauren feels angry and confused. In many ways, she still believes the way she always has, and wants to continue worshiping God. Evangelical Christianity is a part of who she is—but so is being a lesbian. She wants to believe that God does not condemn her for her sexual orientation, but at the same time, she doesn't really know how to think about God anymore. Does God believe she is a sinner, the way her church does?

"Strugglers" with Sexuality and Faith

"You can't be a Jew and be gay."

That's what Joel's older sister Kate told him when he confided in her that he thought he was more attracted to boys than he was to girls.

"So you better get over that right now," Kate continued, "because if Mom finds out, she'll be really upset."

Joel knew his mother wanted all her kids to get married and give her grandchildren. But his oldest sister Judy was thirty-five and still didn't have any children, although she was married. Judy was a lawyer and said she didn't have time for children. Their mother disapproved, fretted, and complained—but it wasn't *that* big of a deal. Would it be that much worse if his parents found out he was homosexual?

Two years later, when Joel was seventeen, he finally revealed to his parents that he was gay. They didn't seem angry, but two weeks later, Joel's mother announced that she had made an appointment for him to see a psychologist. "He's Jewish," she told Joel, "and he works exclusively with people like you, people who are strugglers."

"Strugglers?" Joel didn't think he needed to see a psychologist. He guessed that his mom thought a therapist could help him cope with the stress of coming out as a gay Jewish man.

"That's the word the therapist used," his mother said. "People who are trying to overcome their same-sex attraction so that they can live the Jewish faith. He was very positive. He says he's never had a failure, that all his clients are eventually able to get over their homosexual urges and go on to have happy marriages."

The psychologist was respectful and pleasant, but Joel was too angry to give him a chance. After a few sessions, though, Joel was starting to feel confused. Maybe the guy was right; maybe he *could* stop being attracted to other men. Maybe he *should*.

After a few weeks, Joel went to talk to his **rabbi**. He felt awkward at first, but eventually, he was able to tell the rabbi his whole story. He finished by saying, "I'm not even sure who I am anymore. If I'm gay, then that apparently means I'm not Jewish. I don't want to lose being Jewish. But at the same time, if being Jewish means I can't be gay . . . well, I'm not sure I can handle that either."

The rabbi said, "First of all, Joel, a Jew is a Jew is a Jew. Your identity as a Jew who is entitled to practice your faith does not depend on your sexual feelings or desires or life-partner choices. It simply is so. So let's start with that as our foundation."

Joel found talking with his rabbi far more helpful than talking to the therapist. Eventually, his parents agreed to meet with the rabbi as well. Joel and his family still haven't found an answer that makes everyone happy, but Joel has a new sense of confidence and clarity, knowing that as a gay man he will also always be a Jew.

Gay and Faithful: "Two Parts of Who I Am"

When Faisal Alam's family moved to the United States when he was ten, they remained as devoted to their religion as they had been in their home country. Attending **mosque** was an important part of Faisal's life; being a Muslim was vital to his identity. But at the same time, even as a child, he knew he "wasn't like other boys."

"One of the things that was taught to me at my mosque was that homosexuality is forbidden within Islam," he told the Lansing, Michigan, *City Pulse*. "There's no such thing as a gay Muslim because they just don't exist."

On the outside, at least, Faisal was the model Muslim teenager. When he went to college, he represented the Muslim Student Association in the New England region. Meanwhile, in the city's nightclubs, he had "exploded out of the closet."

Faisal entered a relationship with a young woman and became engaged, but they eventually broke up. When they did, Faisal at last faced the fact that he needed to somehow find a way to heal the break between the two parts of his identity—being Muslim and being gay. "They were both parts of who I was," he says.

Today, Faisal works with other young Muslims who are facing the same issue. He founded Al-Fatiha, an organization dedicated to empowering gay, lesbian, bisexual, and transgender Muslims. "They came to Al-Fatiha trying to find a way back," he says. "It was such a powerful, spiritual experience to be in a space finally that welcomed you as you are. . . ."

Although helping people to reconcile homosexuality with Islam is Faisal's mission in life, he still hasn't completely found his own answers. He doesn't attend mosque, and he considers himself more spiritual than religious. There is still a wound inside him that lies between his gay identity and his Muslim one.

The Rift Between Devotion and Desire

Ekanta looks very much like any American teenager. She wears blue jeans most of the time, and the tiny diamond she wears in her nostril is very fashionable. Her friends tell her that her dark eyes, long shiny hair, and white smile make her beautiful. Boys like her, but Ekanta has never been interested in dating. She likes having fun with her friends, but her religion has always been more important to her. "As a Hindu," she says, "I want to give myself to the Divine. I've wanted this ever since I was a little girl, praying with my grandmother in front of Krishna. This means I will seek self-control. I will give myself in service to others. I always assumed that one day I would marry, but I did not intend to allow sexual attachments to divert me from my pursuit of the Truth."

When Ekanta was eighteen, her parents arranged an engagement for her with an Indian businessman from New Delhi who had recently immigrated to the United States. "He was a little older than me, in his thirties, but that was not a concern for me," Ekanta says. "We were quite compatible. I felt sure I could have a happy life with him because he respected my devotion to my religion. I wanted to go to college, though, so we agreed to wait until I graduated to marry."

At college, however, Ekanta fell in love for the first time—with another woman. "Suddenly," she says, "my whole life has changed. Homosexuality is not the issue so much. For me and my family, homosexuality is an external trait that has nothing to do with your spirit. The *guna*—the character and personality traits—of a person are much more important than any label. If I tell my parents I am a lesbian, they will not be upset with me or condemn me, but they will still expect me to get married. They will not understand why I would not want to now. And what bothers me is that I can no longer look at myself the same. In my heart, I thought I was better than my friends who were always falling in love. I had more control, I was not mired in sexual feelings like they were, I had risen above the physical plain to a purer devotion to the Divine. And now I am forced to admit that is not true. I am a lesbian. It was only because I had not faced that fact that I thought I was so sexually pure. This is upsetting and confusing to me. I do not want to give up my pursuit of Truth. I do not want to give up my lover. I do not know how to put the two together. I do not know if it is possible."

 CLOSE-UP: THE DILEMMA OF MARRIAGE EQUALITY

When the Supreme Court struck down the Defense of Marriage Act in 2015, opening the institution of marriage to all citizens, it was over the objection of many organized religions, including most Christian denominations—who persist in refusing to acknowledge, much less sanctify, civil marriages between LGBT couples. This has resulted in an entirely new difficulty for LGBT believers who had succeeded in finding acceptance and fulfillment in their spiritual communities; in order to marry, they must once again place themselves outside their faiths. For advocates of marriage equality, it seems clear that while the legal struggle may be over, the religious one is still under way. However, there are already signs of progress; Unitarian Universalists have always supported marriage equality—and the Episcopal Church responded to the Supreme Court ruling by changing its laws to allow same-sex religious marriages throughout the denomination, prompting hope that other churches will follow.

"God's Will for You in This Life"

Sunee was born in Thailand and lived there until she was seventeen. Although Sunee has a penis, she thinks of herself as a girl. She has long hair, wears dresses, and carefully puts on her makeup every morning. In Thailand, Sunee was accepted as a member of "the third sex," sometimes referred to as a *kathoey*. She had seen herself as female for as long as she can remember, and her family considers her a girl as well. As devout Buddhists, Sunee's transgender identity was never an issue for them.

When the family moved to the United States, however, all that changed. Sunee had expected Americans to be more **liberal**, but that turned out not to be the case. She had to register for high school as a boy, and word quickly spread that the new Thai girl was actually male. People whispered and giggled behind her back. Sunee spoke English well enough that she could understand what they were saying; she came home and cried in her room every day.

Sunee and her mother went to a Buddhist temple to ask the advice of a priest. He told them, "Everyone has been a member of the third sex in a past life—so the people who are laughing at you were once themselves just like you in another life. All of us have been through innumerable cycles of **reincarnation**. No one can know how many times they have been like you in the past or how many times they will be in the future. To be born as a member of the third sex is the consequence of how we lived a past life."

"So, it is punishment for bad **karma**?" Sunee's mother asked.

The priest nodded, and Sunee's heart sank. "But," he said, "it is not bad karma to live your life as the third sex. It is simply God's will for you in this life. There is no future punishment for it."

After that, Sunee was still unhappy at school, and she did not like thinking that her very identity was punishment for her past sins. "But in some ways," she says, "I did feel better."

When she graduated from high school, she attended Oberlin College, where her transgender identity was once more recognized and affirmed. She is resolved now to have surgery that will bring her physical characteristics into alignment with her identity, and her parents support her decision. She wants to go on to become a doctor, and she hopes that one day she will find a man to marry who will accept her. In the meantime, she says, "My faith gives me strength and peace every day."

Divinity or Identity: Choosing Both

All five of these young people have something important in common: they are all deeply committed to a life of faith. They do not want to live their lives apart from their spiritual beliefs. Their faith is essential not only to how they understand their lives but to their very identities as well. But these individuals also have something else in common: they are all struggling to reconcile their sexuality or gender with their faith.

As our modern culture changes, however, and LGBT identities become more acceptable, increasing numbers of gay and transgender people are refusing to accept that they have to give up their faith. They are taking a fresh look at ancient scriptures and finding that new interpretations are possible. They are starting to ask difficult questions about the difference between faith and culture, between God's perspectives and human perspectives. These are not easy questions to answer.

The issues are a little different for each religious tradition. Even within a given faith, different religious groups believe different things. It can be confusing for LGBT people to find the answers they need to resolve such complex dilemmas.

TEXT-DEPENDENT QUESTIONS

- Is homosexuality compatible with Jewish identity?

- Is homosexuality compatible with Muslim identity?

- What is the Buddhist view of transgender identity?

 RESEARCH PROJECTS

- If you belong to, or were brought up in, a certain faith, find out what its holy texts or scriptures have to say about homosexuality.

- Compare the Christian concept of salvation with the Hindu concept of karma.

- Many organized religions have chapters or groups that welcome, or are designed for, gay people. See if this is true of yours, and note how the group presents and explains itself.

Many organizations are out there supporting and affirming LGBT Christians.

2
CHRISTIANITY

 WORDS TO UNDERSTAND

Celibate: Choosing not to have sex.
Lay people: The people in a church who are not clergy.
Theologians: People who study the nature of God and religious truth.
Monogamous: Having only one sexual partner.
Denominations: Large groups of religious congregations united under a common faith and name, and organized under a single legal administration.
Ordination: The process of becoming a member of the clergy.

Historically, the beliefs of the church regarding homosexuality have been built on what was understood to be the teaching of the Bible, particularly the Old Testament. In reality, until the fall of Rome in 430 A.D., urban culture was tolerant of gay Christians. It wasn't until the organized form Catholicism arrived on the scene that Christians became obsessed with sexual sin.

CLOSE-UP: FROM THE UNIVERSAL TO THE SPECIFIC

The word *Catholic*—from the Greek word for *universal*—was first used in the second century in reference to the entire Christian community. In the sixteenth century, it came to refer to the form of Christianity led by the Pope in Rome, whose authority was supported by layers of bishops and priests.

Historical Catholicism

The Catholic Church has long taught that sexual relations are only acceptable within a marriage and then only for the purpose of conceiving babies. In the Middle Ages (the European era that spanned from the sixth century through the sixteenth century), sexual corruption within the church led its leaders to mandate that priests be **celibate**. Sexual urges were viewed as irrational, destructive—and ultimately sinful—desires, on the same level with anger and greed. **Lay people** were allowed to marry, and sex was permissible within the boundary lines drawn by marriage, but only for the purposes of creating babies.

As a result, Catholicism spoke out strongly against all other sexual acts that could not lead to pregnancy. These included anal sex, oral sex, sex that takes place using any form of birth control—and homosexual intercourse.

Catholicism Today

The official teachings of the Church regarding homosexuality have changed very little over the years. Homosexuality itself is not regarded as a sin, since it is not considered a matter of personal choice—but homosexual *activities* are viewed as evil because they do not produce babies. This has created a wide gap between the official stance of the Vatican and what is believed by many practicing Catholics, especially in the United States (though recently Pope Francis has made overtures at closing the gap by, among other things, chiding the Church fathers for focusing too much of their attention on sexuality matters). According to a recent Gallup poll, 80 percent of American Catholics believe that individuals should not depend on the Church's teachings but must determine for themselves whether homosexuality is moral or immoral.

Many Catholics, including leading **theologians**, have come to believe that sex is a gift from God, intended not only to produce babies but also as an expression of intimacy and committed love. Abusive or demeaning sexual relationships are not what God intended, so sex should be considered a serious and sacred responsibility. Casual sex is not endorsed by this perspective, but any form of **monogamous** sex that expresses the love between two people—including homosexual sex—would be considered a gift from God.

With the affirmation of marriage equality by the U.S. Supreme Court, Christian weddings for LGBT people are legal.

The Protestant Perspective

No Single Point of View

Unlike Catholicism, Protestants have no single unifying hierarchy. There are many Protestant **denominations**, and each one looks at homosexuality a little differently. For example, the United Church of Christ has an official perspective similar to many Catholics' unofficial beliefs. Because homosexuality is not something a person chooses for himself, it cannot be a sin. Homosexual activity should be guided by the same moral rules that apply to heterosexual sex (such as monogamy and faithfulness). Meanwhile, many Presbyterians and Lutherans oppose homosexuality on moral grounds while they actively affirm the civil rights of LGBT people. Many of these churches are politically active, working to end discrimination against same-sex couples. The Church of the Brethren takes a similar stand. Other Protestant denominations, such as the Unity and Universalist churches, believe there is nothing wrong with homosexuality and that homosexuals have the right to be married within the church.

The **ordination** of openly gay people is another issue with which Protestant denominations struggle. The most liberal denominations—those that perform marriages for LGBT people (such as the Unitarians and the United Church of Christ)—have for some time ordained gays. Others, such as the Methodists and Presbyterians, continue to debate the issue. Many gay people serve as ministers in these and all denominations, and must wait patiently for their churches to come to terms with their official recognition.

Evangelical Protestantism

At the other end of the spectrum are conservative Evangelical churches that are actively against all forms of homosexuality. These groups believe that homosexuality is both a choice and a sin. Most of these groups would teach that it is wrong to treat a gay person unkindly, but they would say that homosexuals need to be saved from their sin. This perspective is expressed well by theologian Lehman Strauss:

> *We must always keep before us the fact that homosexuals, like all of us sinners, are the objects of God's love. The Bible says, "But God commendeth His love toward us, in that while we were yet sinners, Christ died for us" (Romans 5:8). . . . The Christian who shares God's love for lost sinners will seek to reach the homosexual with the gospel of Christ, which "is the power of God unto salvation, to every one that believeth" (Romans 1:16). As a Christian I should hate all sin but I can find no justification for hating the sinner. The homosexual is a precious soul for whom Christ died. We Christians can show him the best way of life by pointing him to Christ.*

Finding a Way Forward

Unfortunately, people sometimes use Christianity or other religious doctrines to justify their prejudices. When that happens—when prejudice clothes itself in religion—the true faith, the central meaning that is taught in the scripture, is distorted, if not corrupted. Ultimately, despite their conflicting viewpoints, most Christians are sincerely struggling to interact with the modern world in a spirit of love, being true to what they believe God wants. Their viewpoints on homosexuality, however, differ so much that this issue has become a line that sharply separates groups of Christians, interfering with the unity they claim in the spirit of Christ.

TEXT-DEPENDENT QUESTIONS

- How did the Catholic Church decide which sex acts to forbid?
- In the Catholic view, are homosexual persons and homosexual acts treated equally or differently?
- What is the Protestant position on homosexuality?

 RESEARCH PROJECTS

- Speak to a Catholic priest or nun, and ask how he or she deals with gay parishioners.
- Seek out the same information from a Protestant cleric, and compare the answers.
- Consider the consequences of being an LGBT member of the Catholic Church (whose supreme head, the Pope, can alter the church's policies on his own) versus being an LGBT member of the Protestant Church (which consists of a large number of independent denominations with more democratic processes).

The LGBT synagogue float in the New York City Gay Pride parade.

GAY
TRANSGENDER
BISEXUAL
LESBIAN
QUEER
INTERSEX
STRAIGHT
JEWISH

Beit Simchat Torah CONGREGATION | CBST.ORG

קהלה קדושה בית שמחת תורה

3

JUDAISM

Judaism teaches that sexuality is a powerful force that can be used for both
good and evil. Therefore, sexuality needs to be channeled carefully. Although
procreation is seen as the primary purpose of sex (as it is in Christianity),
Judaism recognizes that sexual intimacy is a healthy source of pleasure.

Historical Judaism and Homosexuality

Traditionally, Judaism has been against homosexuality. In the scriptures,
sexual acts such as incest, masturbation, and homosexuality are often

grouped together as unacceptable, and the **halakah** specifically prohibits same-sex relationships. In later **rabbinic** writings, male homosexuality is condemned, both because it doesn't result in children and because it is viewed as a selfish activity that only gives pleasure to one partner at a time. Male-male intercourse is referred to as an "abhorrence" in the Jewish scriptures.

Meanwhile, the ancient Jewish laws say much less about lesbianism. Because no penetration occurs during female-female sex, women who had had sexual relationships with other women were still considered virgins. This meant they were "pure" and could marry priests.

In general, the Jewish religion treated women as though they were so insignificant as to be invisible; as a result, lesbian relationships were largely ignored. At most, they were referred to as an "obscenity" (a much milder word than "abhorrence"!), but only because lesbian sex involved the woman exposing her naked body to another woman.

 CLOSE-UP: THE LOVE OF RUTH AND NAOMI

The story of Ruth and Naomi is told in the Book of Ruth, which is contained within both the Jewish and Christian scriptures. Naomi is Ruth's mother-in-law, but both their husbands have died. When Naomi decides to go back to her homeland, she tells Ruth to return to her own family as well—but Ruth responds, "Don't ask me to ever leave you . . . for only death will separate me from you."

Liberal Jews believe that God created sex to be a joyful expression of committed love between two people, regardless of their gender.

Modern Judaism and Homosexuality

Today, some Jewish women argue that by ignoring female homosexuals, Judaism is **trivializing** lesbianism—that in effect, to be a lesbian Jew is to be ignored, to have your experience **invalidated**. "How can you embrace a religion where your central experience is dismissed as merely a minor infraction?" asks one woman.

As with Christianity, different Jewish groups look at homosexuality differently. Orthodox Jews still hold on to the traditional perspectives on homosexuality. This means that if a person comes out as gay, he may very well have to leave his religious community and become estranged from his family. Meanwhile, within Conservative Judaism, LGBT Jews are generally accepted; however, while some groups ordain gay rabbis and even perform same-sex blessings, others do not or will only ordain gay rabbis who commit to being celibate.

Within Reform Judaism, gays and lesbians are respected, openly gay people are ordained as rabbis, and Reform rabbis perform commitment ceremonies and weddings for gay and lesbian couples.

 CLOSE-UP: JUDAISM AND TRANSGENDER PEOPLE

Orthodox Judaism is surprisingly inconclusive about transgender issues. While Deuteronomy forbids cross-dressing and any other behaviors that identify an individual with the opposite sex, some Orthodox authorities permit gender affirmation surgery. Conservative Judaism is equally unresolved on the issue, though Alviva Kapor, a rabbi ordained in 2005, began living as a woman in 2012—the first transgender female rabbi in history. Reform and Reconstructionist Judaism are more accepting and welcoming of transgender issues and gender nonconformity.

Many liberal Jews are taking another look at the scripture and finding new meanings in many of the stories. The story of Ruth and Naomi, for example, is viewed as an example of committed love between two women.

For most Jews who accept homosexuality, monogamy is the more important issue. They believe that God created the sex act to be a joyful expression of committed love between two people, regardless of their gender.

 TEXT-DEPENDENT QUESTIONS

- What is the principle difference between the traditional Jewish view of sex and the conservative Christian view of it?
- Why were Jewish lesbians seen with less disfavor than were gay men?
- Which Jewish tradition is most welcoming to LGBT people?

 RESEARCH PROJECTS

- Interview rabbis from various Jewish traditions (Orthodox, Conservative, or Reform) about their views on homosexuality.
- Watch the movie *Trembling Before G-d*, a documentary about gay Orthodox Jews struggling to reconcile their sexuality with their faith.
- Visit some websites catering to LGBT Jews, such as Keshet (keshetonline.org) and Nehirim (nehirim.org), and check out the issues and topics they cover.

LGBT Muslims can be
devout and out.

4

ISLAM

The Qur'an, or Muslim holy book, clearly condemns homosexuality. Many traditional Muslims connect this issue to the story of Lot (a story that also appears in Christian and Jewish scripture). In the story, God lets Lot leave his home in the town of Sodom before it is destroyed. One interpretation of the story in the Muslim (and some Christian) traditions explains that the city is destroyed because the people in it are practicing homosexuality. There are other interpretations as well, but this version makes the connection with gays and lesbians being referred to as *Luti*, or "Lot's people." The story of Lot is mentioned five times throughout the Qur'an.

Part of the reason why Islam views homosexuality as sinful is that sex is understood to be for the purpose of procreation—for making children. Sexual activity is therefore encouraged and even sacred; there is no tradition of celibacy in Islam as there is in Christianity or other religions.

Homosexuality in Modern Islamic Culture

Today, homosexuality remains punishable by *shari'a*, Islamic law. In some Muslim countries, the punishment is a death sentence. However, solid evidence must be provided before punishment occurs, and most Muslims aren't that concerned with what others do in their private lives. As long as homosexuality occurs in private, realistically, it cannot be punished.

This affects how people in the Islamic world, and even Muslims here in the United States, label themselves. As a Muslim, it's not so bad to have sex with someone of the same gender as long as you don't proclaim yourself as gay and take on a homosexual identity.

Many conservative Muslims see the label of "homosexuality" as a sign of Western culture and its influence on Islamic ways of life. These people would argue that there was no label before the West got involved—people did what they wanted in private, but they would eventually become part of a heterosexual marriage, and no one felt the need to proclaim themselves as "gay."

This understanding of homosexual behavior has both its pros and cons. On the plus side, it frees people to act in any way they choose in

CLOSE-UP: ISLAM AND TRANSGENDER PEOPLE

Traditional Islam does not deal directly with the subject of transgender people. The one passage in an Islamic religious text that seems to touch on the issue is a *hadith* (a story about the Prophet Mohammed) that seems to argue against cross-dressing, saying, "cursed are those men who wear women's clothing and those women who wear men's clothing." This story aside, transgender people tend to be accepted within Islam more than homosexual people are.

In 1988, Islamic law declared that gender affirmation surgery was acceptable. In Egypt, the highest religious leader in the country issued a decree that such surgery was permissible and even encouraged in cases where a patient was truly transgender and unable to live a full life as the gender he or she was assigned at birth. However, the decree went on to proclaim that surgery for the "mere wish" of changing one's gender is not permitted.

Other Muslim countries have also responded positively toward transgender individuals. In Malaysia, the government has accepted transgender people for years and is amenable to reissuing government documents to people who have adopted new gender identities. Pakistan includes a third gender option on government documents. And Iran in 2004 officially recognized transgender individuals, allowing them to have gender affirmation surgery and to get new official documents.

private, as long as they are willing to conform to Muslim codes of behavior in public. But many gay Muslims, especially in the United States, feel that hiding who they are is not an acceptable way to live. Keeping up a public appearance of heterosexuality, they say, denies that a part of them really exists.

Now that the Gay Rights movements and other Western influences have gained so much attention all around the world, Muslims who are LGBT are beginning to show pride in their identities. They want to come out of the closet—or feel that they *should* come out—and when they do, they run into trouble with the traditions of their religious background.

LGBT muslims are more visible than ever before.

Islam and the Issue of Marriage Equality

Because homosexuality is evil according to the Qur'an—so bad that God destroyed an entire town over homosexual behavior—marriage equality is not supported by many Muslims. Instead, they believe that because the purpose of marriage is to produce children, a true marriage can only exist between a man and a woman.

However, many liberal Muslims are reinterpreting other passages in the Scripture that seem to point to a more **inclusive** idea of relationships, and they use these as a justification for marriage equality. For example, in some parts of the *Qur'an* that talk about the nature of relationships between people, the word used to describe the individuals—*zaui*—is not gendered; instead, it means one half of a partnership. This word has been used as evidence that human partnerships can be between people of the same gender as well as between a man and a woman.

 CLOSE-UP: THE TRADITION OF GAY ARAB POETRY

Despite Islam's condemnation of homosexuality, gay love and relationships occasionally occur in Islamic art—and in a long tradition of gay-themed poetry, beginning with the work of Abu Nuwas (756-814) and including Muhammad al-Nawaji (1383-1455), who wrote:

God! How beautiful, this young
Cucumber seller, and a face to make
The sun itself blush at noontime.
The day he agreed to a tender meeting
I was overwhelmed.
Ah, how I savored
That mouth of cucumber

Gay and Lesbian Muslims in the United States

In 2008, the San Francisco Gay Pride parade included a Muslim float for the first time. However, unlike the rest of the crowd, who were openly embracing their identities as LGBT people, the Muslim gay men on the float hid behind sunglasses and hats. While Islam tends to be more liberal in the United States than in Muslim countries such as Egypt or Afghanistan, it is still hard for American Muslims to come out and publicly proclaim a homosexual identity.

Fortunately, this is slowly changing. Many Muslim **advocates** for LGBT rights argue that the Qur'an emphasizes that all people are God's creation. Everyone is equally loved and cared for by God, no matter what their sexuality. Some people also argue that while the Qur'an forbids "abominations" when it comes to same-sex relations, it doesn't specify exactly what these abominations are. All scripture is open to interpretation, and the Qur'an can be interpreted in a more inclusive light.

Some LGBT Muslims draw on alternative traditions within Islam that rely less on Scripture and Islamic Law. One such tradition is Sufism, a **mystical** tradition within Islam that stresses personal experience and relationship with God.

TEXT-DEPENDENT QUESTIONS

- Why are gay people known in Islam as *Luti*?

- What is the difference, in Muslim culture, between public and private homosexual behavior?

- Is the Islamic view of transgender identity the same as its view of homosexuality?

 RESEARCH PROJECTS

- Check out the writings of LGBT Muslims advocating for reform, such as Irshad Manji (irshadmanji.com).

- Islam, Christianity, and Judaism all share certain texts; compare and contrast the views they derive from them on same-sex behavior, sexual pleasure, and sexual identity.

- Compare the status of LGBT people in different Islamic countries—from Turkey and Malaysia to Iran and Saudi Arabia.

In India, *hijra*, the "third sex," is an accepted group.

5

HINDUISM

 WORDS TO UNDERSTAND

Caste: A Hindu hereditary social class. If you are born into a low or high caste, it will remain your status for your entire life. (Although the caste system is weakening in Hindu culture, it is still uncommon for people to marry outside their own caste.)

Materialistic: Excessively concerned with material things, such as possessions and money.

Sects: Subdivisions of larger religious groups that usually differ in some way from the rest of the religion.

According to Harvard University's Pluralism Project, more than 1.2 million Hindus live in the United States today, but that label includes a vast range of beliefs. Unlike monotheistic religions—including Christianity, Judaism, and Islam—Hinduism has no central doctrine that tells people what to believe. Some Hindus believe in many gods, whereas others believe in no god at all. Some practice daily meditation, and others offer sacrifices, called *pujas*, to their household images of the gods. Some believe that sexuality is an important part of human experience, while others tend more toward asceticism, the practice of giving up all bodily pleasures. Thus, discussing

Hinduism and homosexuality can be difficult because every Hindu practitioner has his or her own ideas about what Hinduism is.

The Laws of Manu

The Laws of Manu are a collection of teachings written in India sometime between 200 BCE and 200 CE. They deal with people's *dharma*, or duty; every individual, depending on gender and **caste**, has a specific *dharma* that must be fulfilled. The Laws of Manu describe these duties and list appropriate punishments for failing to obey them—and under these laws, homosexuality is considered a crime.

However, some modern Hindus and scholars argue that the punishments are light—and that therefore homosexuality shouldn't be considered all that

 CLOSE-UP: THE THIRD SEX

In Hindu culture, all people are considered to have both male and female parts to their personalities. Some men, however, embody more of the "feminine"—and they are seen as neither male nor female. Members of this "third sex" are referred to in India as *hijra*. Some of the *hijra* are born with both male and female sexual organs, while others are born with male sexual organs and may or may not undergo gender affirmation surgery. Whatever sex they were assigned at birth, all of the *hijra* wear traditional women's clothing and are referred to by feminine pronouns such as *she, her,* and *hers*.

In traditional Indian society, the *hijra* occupy specific roles. They often perform at births and marriages, and it is important to pay them well; it is believed that their blessing will enable a child to be successful in life—and that anyone who is cursed by a *hijra* will be unlucky.

In some Hindu **sects**, transvestitism (cross-dressing) is a way to show devotion to god. Men dress up as women to simulate marriage to Siva, and both homosexual behavior and transvestitism can be seen as honoring the gods.

terrible. For example, within the Laws, if two men were caught engaging in homosexual behavior, they were sentenced to bathe with their clothes on—a punishment that seems uncomfortable, possibly embarrassing, but hardly the end of the world. Sexual acts between two women were seen in a stricter light; the punishment for an older woman engaging in sexual relations with a virgin was to have her head shaved, two fingers cut off, and be forced to ride through town on a donkey. (Some people argue that the severity of that particular punishment had more to do with the fact that one woman was a virgin, as women were supposed to remain pure for marriage.)

While homosexuality was cautioned against in the Laws, many Hindu traditions allow for a degree of flexibility in sexuality and gender. For example, in many Hindu religious traditions, one's *kama*, or bodily pleasure, is seen as equally important as one's duty, or *dharma*. In the *Kama Sutra*, an ancient book that provides directions for embracing one's *kama*, sexual behavior is portrayed as enjoyable and meaningful, whether between individuals of the same or different genders.

Being Hindu and Gay

Many modern Hindus believe that homophobia was introduced into their religion by other cultures, especially the British back in the 1700s, when they colonized India. Before that time, homosexuality was rarely dealt with in public but was commonly understood as natural. When the British came to India, however, they instituted rigid punishments for homosexual acts. In the Indian Penal Code, which was written by the British, "carnal intercourse against the order of nature" is still punishable by life in prison.

A group of transgender young people attend the Holi Festival. Holi, the ancient festival of colors, is celebrated by spreading colored powders on yourself and others.

 CLOSE-UP: THE FIRESTORM OVER *FIRE*

The film *Fire* came out in India in 1996 and led to riots by fundamentalist Hindus because of its portrayal of two women in a lesbian relationship. Conservative Hindus argued that not only was it wrong to promote lesbian love, but also that the film was poking fun at Hinduism itself, as the main characters—Sita and Radha—were named after important Hindu deities. On the other hand, LGBT activists argued that the film didn't go far enough in portraying lesbian issues for Indian women. They complained that the movie implied that the women became lesbians because they were unfulfilled sexually in their heterosexual relationships. They also felt that it portrayed homosexuality as having been brought to India by the British—a result of listening to Western music or wearing blue jeans.

Today, devout Hindus regard sexuality in several different ways. One popular view argues that physical desires, whether homosexual or heterosexual, are to be avoided. Physical desire leads to a continuation of rebirths, or reincarnation. From this perspective, since the goal of existence is to escape the world we live in now and move past the cycle of reincarnation, one must escape the need for physical pleasure. This concept is not easy for mainstream Americans to grasp. Hindus who follow this path believe that all the things we own and all our relationships are really meaningless; they tie us down to this material world, and so we should learn to view them as unimportant. In our **materialistic** society, this viewpoint may make little sense, but a positive aspect of this worldview is that souls are not seen as male or female; instead, everyone is equal. Many Hindus believe that marriage is the union of two souls—and since souls aren't male or female, what does it matter if the marriage is between two women or two men?

 ## TEXT-DEPENDENT QUESTIONS

- What is the Hindu concept of *dharma*?
- What is the Hindu concept of *kama*?
- In Hindu belief, how does sexuality affect reincarnation?

RESEARCH PROJECTS

- Find an online source for the Laws of Manu, and compare the treatment of homosexuality in the two major Hindu countries, India and Nepal.
- Watch the film *Fire*.

Buddhism portrays relationships between people of the same sex more intimately than different-sex relationships.

6

BUDDHISM

 WORDS TO UNDERSTAND

Monastic: A way of life where people live in seclusion, take religious
vows, and follow a fixed set of rules regulating how they spend their
time. Christians, Buddhists, and Hindus all have monastic orders
whose basic goal is to achieve greater spiritual purity by withdrawing
from the world's distractions.
Penance: An act performed to show sorrow for sin or wrongdoing.
Homoerotic: Having to do with homosexual love and desire.
Novices: People who have entered a religious order but not yet taken
final vows.

Buddhism developed from Hinduism, and like Hinduism it has no over-
arching religious institution or doctrine. The practices and beliefs of
Buddhists differ from country to country, as well as among different
branches of the religion. This means that a Buddhist in the United States
might have different beliefs and practices from a Buddhist in Thailand,
India, or China.

In many Buddhist contexts, homosexuality is pretty much a non-is-
sue. Because until recently Buddhism was a religion practiced mainly

outside the United States, its followers didn't think about sexuality the same way Americans do.

Instead, one of the main conflicts in Buddhism has always been sexuality versus celibacy. Many Buddhists believe that a **monastic** life, where a person is entirely celibate, is the ideal, a state of being that leads more easily to the central goal of the religion: ridding one's self of all desire (much as in some branches of Hinduism). From this perspective, all sex and sexual desire (whether heterosexual or homosexual) only lead one away from this goal. While sex is considered necessary and important for those not in religious orders, monks and nuns are forbidden to engage in sex of any kind. That said, the punishment for homosexual acts is not serious—it simply involves doing acts of **penance**, not something drastic like being expelled from the community.

Historical Buddhism and Homosexuality

The *jatakas* are sacred stories about the Buddha's life, meant to teach his followers how to act. Today, many people argue that some of these stories imply that Buddha and some of his companions had homosexual relationships. For example, one of Buddha's followers, Ananda, is his constant companion and adviser. Whether or not the Buddha and Ananda were actually engaged in a sexual relationship, theirs and other friendships are portrayed intimately, more so than relationships between members of opposite sexes. The point seems to be that relationships between men and women, whether sexual or nonsexual, can tempt people to leave a religious community, while same-sex relationships don't do this, nor do they result in children. (Family life was seen as lesser than life in a religious community.) This is very different from the Christian and Jewish perspectives!

So, at worst, historical Buddhism was neutral toward homosexuality, while at best it actively encouraged it. As a result, in some branches of Buddhism, homosexuality has been practiced regularly. In Japan, for example, a tradition of **homoerotic** literature and poetry dates back to the fourteenth century CE. In these stories, older monks took younger **novices** as lovers as a way to teach the young monks about the practices of their religion. Clearly, from this perspective, homosexuality was not perceived as either sinful or destructive.

Buddhism, like Hinduism, sees gender as a fluid quality. Here, in this painting from a Buddhist monastery in Laos, Lord Buddha is portrayed with feminine characteristics.

CLOSE-UP: BUDDHISM AND TRANSGENDER PEOPLE

Because Buddhism views our physical life on Earth as something temporary and inferior, both male and female characteristics are considered to be transitory—things that will pass away with our present bodies. In other words, our souls are genderless; they just happen to be housed in a body with a specific sex. So, as with Hindus, many Buddhists are comfortable with gender flexibility.

One of the texts that describes the rules for Buddhist monks and nuns, called the *Vinaya Pitaka*, tells about two people—one male and one female—who go through a sex change. The Buddha allows them to live as their new genders within monastic religious communities. Stories like this one provide important support for Buddhists going through gender transitions today.

Buddhism in the United States Today

Because of its history of tolerance, many LGBT Americans convert to Buddhism, seeing it as a much more accepting community than the religions in which they were raised. Its philosophy and perspective can be helpful to young adults struggling with their religious identity.

In Conclusion

Some people would say that much of how we think about sexuality and gender has more to do with culture than with biology—or morality. Others believe very strongly that their religion's absolute code of right and wrong rules out homosexuality as an acceptable behavior. It is a difficult issue, and in today's world, religious people from many faiths are struggling with it.

What do you think?

 TEXT-DEPENDENT QUESTIONS

- Do Buddhists consider homosexuality to be sinful?
- What do many Buddhists view as the ideal sexual lifestyle?
- What is the Buddhist response to monks or nuns who violate their sexual vows?

 RESEARCH PROJECTS

- Like most major religions, Buddhism strives to combine sexuality and spirituality. List a few ways in which its methods differ from Christianity, Judaism, Islam, and Hinduism.
- Talk to a Buddhist monk or nun, and ask about the ways they incorporate their sexuality into their faith.
- Weigh everything you've read, and decide which religion you think would be most welcoming and encouraging to someone who is LGBT.

▣ SERIES GLOSSARY

Activists: People committed to social change through political and personal action.

Advocacy: The process of supporting the rights of a group of people and speaking out on their behalf.

Alienation: A feeling of separation and distance from other people and from society.

Allies: People who support others in a cause.

Ambiguous: Something unclear or confusing.

Anonymous: Being unknown; having no one know who you are.

Assumption: A conclusion drawn without the benefit of real evidence.

Backlash: An adverse reaction by a large number of people, especially to a social or political development.

Bias: A tendency or preference toward a particular perspective or ideology that interferes with the ability to be impartial, unprejudiced, or objective.

Bigotry: Stubborn and complete intolerance of a religion, appearance, belief, or ethnic background that differs from one's own.

Binary: A system made up of two, and only two, parts.

Bohemian: Used to describe movements, people, or places characterized by nontraditional values and ways of life often coupled with an interest in the arts and political movements.

Caricature: An exaggerated representation of a person.

Celibate: Choosing not to have sex.

Chromosome: A microscopic thread of genes within a cell that carries all the information determining what a person is like, including his or her sex.

Cisgender: Someone who self-identifies with the gender he or she was assigned at birth.

Civil rights: The rights of a citizen to personal and political freedom under the law.

Clichés: Expressions that have become so overused—stereotypes, for example—that they tend to be used without thought.

Closeted: Choosing to conceal one's true sexual orientation or gender identity.

Compensating: Making up for something by trying harder or going further in the opposite direction.

Conservative: Cautious; resistant to change and new ideas.

Controversy: A disagreement, often involving a touchy subject about which differing opinions create tension and strong reactions.

Customs: Ideas and ways of doing things that are commonly understood and shared within a society.

Demonize: Portray something or someone as evil.

Denominations: Large groups of religious congregations united under a common faith and name, and organized under a single legal administration.

Derogatory: Critical or cruel, as in a term used to make a person feel devalued or humiliated.

Deviation: Something abnormal; something that has moved away from the standard.

Dichotomy: Division into two opposite and contradictory groups.

Discrimination: When someone is treated differently because of his or her race, sexual orientation, gender identity, religion, or some other factor.

Disproportionate: A situation where one particular group is overrepresented within a larger group.

Diverse: In the case of a community, one that is made up of people from many different backgrounds.

Effeminate: A word used to refer to men who have so-called feminine qualities.

Emasculated: Having had one's masculinity or manhood taken away.

Empathy: Feeling for another person; putting yourself mentally and emotionally in another person's place.

Empirical evidence: Factual data gathered from direct observation.

Empowering: Providing strength and energy; making someone feel powerful.

Endocrinologist: A medical doctor who specializes in the treatment of hormonal issues.

Epithets: Words or terms used in a derogatory way to put a person down.

The Establishment: The people who hold influence and power in society.

Extremist: Someone who is in favor of using extreme or radical measures, especially in politics and religion.

Flamboyant: Colorful and a bit outrageous.

Fundamentalist: Someone who believes in a particular religion's fundamental principles and follows them rigidly. When the word is used in connection with Christianity, it refers to a member of a form of Protestant Christianity that believes in the strict and literal interpretation of the Bible.

Gay liberation: The movement for the civil and legal rights of gay people that originated in the 1950s and emerged as a potent force for social and political change in the late 1960s and '70s.

Gender: A constructed sexual identity, whether masculine, feminine, or entirely different.

Gender identity: A person's self-image as female, male, or something entirely different, no matter what gender a person was assigned at birth.

Gender roles: Those activities and traits that are considered appropriate to males and females within a given culture.

Gene: A microscopic sequence of DNA located within a chromosome that determines a particular biological characteristic, such as eye color.

Genitalia: The scientific term for the male and female sex organs.

Genocide: The large-scale murder and destruction of a particular group of people.

Grassroots: At a local level; usually used in reference to political action that begins within a community rather than on a national or global scale.

Harassed/harassment: Being teased, bullied, or physically threatened.

Hate crime: An illegal act in which the victim is targeted because of his or her race, religion, sexual orientation, or gender identity.

Homoerotic: Having to do with homosexual, or same-sex, love and desire.

Homophobia: The fear and hatred of homosexuality. A homophobic person is sometimes referred to as a "homophobe."

Horizontal hostility: Negative feeling among people within the same minority group.

Hormones: Chemicals produced by the body that regulate biological functions, including male and female gender traits, such as beard growth and breast development.

Identity: The way a person, or a group of people, defines and understands who they are.

Inborn: Traits, whether visible or not, that are a part of who we are at birth.

Inclusive: Open to all ideas and points of view.

Inhibitions: Feelings of guilt and shame that keep us from doing things we might otherwise want to do.

Internalized: Taken in; for example, when a person believes the negative opinions other people have of him, he has *internalized* their point of view and made it his own.

Interpretation: A particular way of understanding something.

Intervention: An organized effort to help people by changing their attitudes or behavior.

Karma: The force, recognized by both Hindus and Buddhists, that emanates from one's actions in this life; the concept that the good and bad things one does determine where he or she will end up in the next life.

Legitimized: Being taken seriously and having the support of large numbers of people.

LGBT: An initialism that stands for lesbian, gay, bisexual, and transgender. Sometimes a "Q" is added (**LGBTQ**) to include "questioning." "Q" may also stand for "queer."

Liberal: Open to new ideas; progressive; accepting and supportive of the ideas or identity of others.

Liberation: The act of being set free from oppression and persecution.

Mainstream: Accepted, understood, and supported by the majority of people.

Malpractice: When a doctor or other professional gives bad advice or treatment, either out of ignorance or deliberately.

Marginalize: Push someone to the sidelines, away from the rest of the world.

Mentor: Someone who teaches and offers support to another, often younger, person.

Monogamous: Having only one sexual or romantic partner.

Oppress: Keep another person or group of people in an inferior position.

Ostracized: Excluded from the rest of a group.

Out: For an LGBT person, the state of being open with other people about his or her sexual orientation or gender identity.

Outed: Revealed or exposed as LGBT against one's will.

Persona: A character or personality chosen by a person to change the way others perceive them.

Pioneers: People who are the first to try new things and experiment with new ways of life.

Politicized: Aware of one's rights and willing to demand them through political action.

Prejudice: An opinion (usually unfavorable) of a person or a group of people not based on actual knowledge.

Proactive: Taking action taken in advance of an anticipated situation or difficulty.

Progressive: Supporting human freedom and progress.

Psychologists and psychiatrists: Professionals who study the human mind and human behavior. Psychiatrists are medical doctors who can prescribe pills, whereas clinical psychologists provide talk therapy.

Quackery: When an untrained person gives medical advice or treatment, pretending to be a doctor or other medical expert.

The Right: In politics and religion, the side that is generally against social change and new ideas; often used interchangeably with *conservative*.

Segregation: Historically, a system of laws and customs that limited African Americans' access to many businesses, public spaces, schools, and neighborhoods that were "white only."

Sexual orientation: A person's physical and emotional attraction to the opposite sex (heterosexuality), the same sex (homosexuality), both sexes (bisexuality), or neither (asexuality).

Sociologists: People who study the way groups of humans behave.

Spectrum: A wide range of variations.

Stereotype: A caricature; a way to judge someone, probably unfairly, based on opinions you may have about a particular group they belong to.

Stigma: A mark of shame.

Subculture: A smaller group of people with similar interests and lifestyles within a larger group.

Taboo: Something that is forbidden.

Theories: Ideas or explanations based on research, experimentation, and evidence.

Tolerance: Acceptance of, and respect for, other people's differences.

Transgender: People who identify with a gender different from the one they were assigned at birth.

Transphobia: Fear or hatred of transgender people.

Variance: A range of differences within a category such as gender.

Victimized: Subjected to unfair and negative treatment, including violence, bullying, harassment, or prejudice.

FURTHER RESOURCES

Hartford Institute for Religion Research
Articles and research on the intersection of homosexuality and religion.
hirr.hartsem.edu/research/homosexuality_religion.html

Religious Tolerance
Individual religious groups' policies and beliefs about homosexuality.
www.religioustolerance.org/hom_chur.htm

DignityUSA
DignityUSA seeks to bring together LGBT Catholics and work toward a more inclusive Church.
www.dignityusa.org

The Reformation Project
Grassroots organization hosting training sessions and reaching out to Christian leaders.
www.reformationproject.org

Truth Wins Out
Exposés on the leading ministries from Truth Wins Out, a non-profit organization that works to demolish the foundation of anti-gay prejudice.
www.truthwinsout.org/learn-about-ex-gay-ministries/

Homosexuality and Christianity
Links to articles and essay from a liberal perspective.
www.jeramyt.org/gay.html

Jewish Law Blog
A legal commentary by Richard Greenberg.
www.jlaw.com/Commentary/homosexuality.html

Nehrim
A national community of LGBT Jews, families, and allies, committed to a more just and inclusive world.
www.nehirim.org

Keshet
Working for the full equality and inclusion of LGBT Jews in Jewish life.
www.keshetonline.org

Hinduism and Homosexuality
Background, opposing viewpoints, and debates.
www.religionfacts.com/hinduism/homosexuality

Galva-108
The Gay and Lesbian Vaishnava Association, Inc.
www.galva108.org

Imaan
UK-based support group for LGBT muslims.
www.imaan.org.uk

BuddhaNet
An explanation of homosexuality within Therevadan Buddhism by A. L. DeSilva.
www.buddhanet.net/homosexu.htm

INDEX